QUICK GUIDE TO REAL ESTATE

ESSENTIALS FOR
NEW AGENTS & INVESTORS

Russ H. Carrington IV

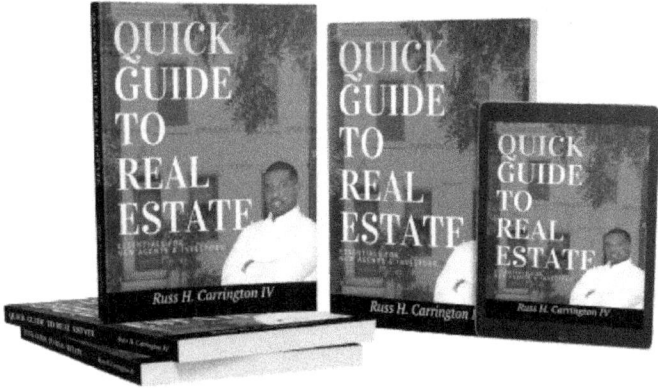

Email: askrusscarrington@gmail.com

Front cover image by Brittany Harper

Book design by Ask Russ Publishing Co., LLC

Ask Russ Publishing Co., LLC Baltimore, MD 21206

www.askrusscarrington.com

TABLE OF CONTENTS

INTRODUCTION

The idea of pre-construction investments is a clever way to make millions.

The theory is really simple. Investing in Real Estate when it's in the planning stages is a great option. Most new construction builders need money to get their projects off ground.

By investing in pre-construction, namely condo units in high demand areas, before the ground is broken investors often have the option to invest pennies on the dollar. Investors can re-sell the property at full market value once the building is complete. Investors will pocket the difference in the original investment and the asking price.

This is a win-win situation for many builders, because 'pre-selling' allows bankers to have confidence in the viability of the project as a moneymaker.

This style of investing is not nearly as glamorous as flipping houses. There is no beast to beauty renovations. There are, however, some things that should be kept in mind while making this type of transaction.

First, no real estate venture is ever guaranteed to turn a profit, no matter what the glossy little brochures tell you. You have to keep your eye on current real estate sales in your target market. Markets change regularly in this space.

Secondly, networking is more often than not the best way to break into this particular business. There are all kinds of fly by night, would be real estate investors. The ones that manage to turn a profit are those that network with other real estate agents who have specific interests in pre-construction investments. Join local real estate groups in addition to online groups that deal specifically with these sorts of investments.

The costs involved might appear daunting at first, but it's far less costly then getting in over your head by not having a grasp of even the most basic 'ins' and 'outs' of pre-construction real estate investing.

Thirdly, develop a close-knit relationship with a Realtor that specializes in this particular type of real estate investing. This could prove to be the most beneficial thing you will ever do to ensure your success. Developing the right relationship with the right Realtor can get you information on new properties before they make it to the public sector.

This puts you in the rare and wonderful position of beating the competition to the punch. This gives you a much better shot at receiving the rock bottom prices that are often missed by waiting too long to make the purchase.

Fourthly, be prepared retain the property if need be. The problem with preconstruction investing is that there are no guarantees. When the time comes you'll been able to 'seal the deal'. Issues come up even when you have a buyer that is willing and eager to make the purchase.

In other words, there are times when you will need to hold onto the property for a while and sometimes as a long-term investment. In some circumstances long-term holds would include renting the property out as an Air BNB if it is in a high demand tourist area. You can use a Realtor to help with that. This allows the property to be earning some income until the sale can be made.

Some investors may decide to hold onto there property as a personal vacation home for themselves. In the end, the important thing is that there is a "Plan B" for your investment.

Pre-construction real estate investing may not have its 'name in lights', but it appeals to some investors, and provides a viable investment style that has the potential to bring in significant profits. The name of the game is "profit." Thus, keep this in mind when considering your investment options. This is one of the forms of investing that requires the least amount of capital upfront.

CHAPTER 1: WHAT TO DO WHEN YOUR HOME ISN'T SELLING

When selling your home, the process is almost like going to a job interview. Selling a home involves presentation, which is one of the key factors that determine the outcome.

Although this may sound a bit weird, presentation is a way of life in real estate. Buyers in today's market look for a good presentation, many base their final decisions on it.

If the property you are selling comes with a garage, you'll need to go through your garage before you place your home on the market. Chances are that you store things in your garage, which can easily pile up over time.

If your garage is full of clutter, you'll want to make it presentable. Buyers look for homes that are in perfect condition, and anything less than perfect is considered less desirable to the buyer.

Most homes have some truly outstanding features. You should always do your best to highlight the best features of your home, instead of hoping that the buyer understands what they are. The ideal way to bring out the best features of your home is to use the proper lighting.

Once your home is de-cluttered, you can use bright lighting to bring out the best features in your home, and ensure that they stand out to the buyer.

When a potential buyers pulls up to your home; the first thing they will see is your lawn. If your lawn is trimmed and well-manicured, they will get a great first impression right off the bat. If your lawn is a less than, they may just pull right away. To give the best impression to the buyer, you should put thought into how things look. Consider planting flowers around the walkway and throughout the yard. These small touches will look great to a potential buyer.

You should also make sure that the entrance into your home is attractive as well. Your entrance area should have appeal also.

You can add some plants, paintings, and rugs to ensure that every potential buyer gets a great impression. When buyer's walk through the entryway of your home, you should make sure the view is a good one. The biggest goal when showing your home is to ensure that the buyer have a great first impression.

Keep in mind that it may take some time to sell your home. These days, there are only two reasons that any house doesn't sell "Price or Access!" If you are having trouble selling your home, check your showing restrictions. If your property is only available to be shown during certain hours, or only on weekend. This could reduce or even stall your sale. Over pricing is a deal killer. Eventually, you will sell your home - although it may take more time.

CHAPTER 2: THINGS TO KNOW BEFORE BUYING A HOME

If you are taking the next step in life and purchasing a home, chances are that you are feeling the pressure and the anxiety that goes along with this difficult decision.

Homes buyers are very anxious, eager to get any information they can about real estate. Before buying a home, it helpful to learn all that you can.

The first thing you'll need to do when buying a home is to find out just how much you qualify for or can afford to borrow. You should also make it a point to check your credit and know where you stand. If you have any problems, you should start correcting them before you attempt to meet with a loan officer. The higher the credit rating, the lower your interest rates will be.

You should attempt to get pre-approved by a mortgage broker or lender, this will show your commitment to the mortgage. Also, make sure to look for any payment or prepayment options that can help you take a few years away from your mortgage. Once you have been pre-approved for a mortgage and know where you stand with your monthly payments, you can start shopping for a home.

When you shop for a home, you should only buy real estate that is perfect for you. Before you start looking, you should always make a list of everything you want your home to have, based on what you want and what you need. You should also make sure that you mark out any areas that you are willing to come to a compromise on, just in case you have to.

To assist you in finding the perfect home, you should enlist the services of a reputable real estate agent. When you meet with your Realtor, you will go over how much you are willing to spend, and what type of home you are looking for. Your agent will know where ideal properties are located, and help you find the home that is best for you.

Your Realtor will supply you with a list of potential properties that meet your budget and your desired amenities. Once you get the list, you should drive by the homes and check out both the home and the neighborhood. You should consider the appearance and location of the home, safety, access to the freeway, schools nearby, commute time to work, local shopping, and even recreational activities.

If you don't find something that interests you the first time, you should keep looking until you find the home that is best for you. Your Realtor can help with tours of homes and such, even tell you information about neighborhoods that you aren't familiar with. If you have chosen a good Realtor, he will care about helping you find a home and go out of their way to ensure that you get exactly what you want.

CHAPTER 3: SELLING REAL ESTATE IN A SLUGGISH MARKET

Real estate is one commodity that many depend upon to get them through the rough times in their investment strategies.

The problem is that unlike stocks and bonds, real estate is not the most liquid of assets to turn into cash when the going gets rough and money gets tight. This may be the one large drawback when it comes to real estate. You cannot rely solely upon real estate to get you through the financially hard time.

There is only one way in which real estate can truly be sold in a sluggish market. However, by offering exceptional value to consumers, you can manage to sell real estate.

This is not the best method of choice for investors. Investors are often encouraged to hold onto properties during the rough times. They are hoping to achieve at least ROI – 'Return on Investment.' When this is not possible, make sure the property being sold based on current market comparable.

Play up the attributes of any given property or offer several properties for sale at once. More importantly, offer different types of properties rather than one style of property. If you own a few rentals, a couple of vacation homes, timeshares, and perhaps a corporate office building, put one of each on the market and see which sells more quickly.

Another thing that must be considered in a sluggish market is that you cannot attach an emotional value to the price of the property. No matter how much sweat, tears, and blood you have vested into the property you must realize that it is a business transaction for you, as it is for the person placing the bid. You cannot afford to run off potential bidders by becoming insulting or feeling insulted by their bids.

Make a counteroffer and see what happens rather than letting emotion rule the day. When it's a buyer's market, there will be low offers.

Many make a living by buying low and selling high. This means they will make an insultingly low offer the first time around to see where the seller stands.

Do not take their actions personally. They are not insulting you or the property only attempting to gain the most money in the process. Most businesses operate this way no matter what they claim.

Selling a property in a sluggish market can be a disappointing and gut-wrenching process. Unexpected expenses arise and money is needed when it is needed. This is why we make these investments in the first place, to be able to handle the unexpected twists and turns that life tosses our way.

CHAPTER 4: TERMITE DAMAGE AND REAL ESTATE

Termite damage, no matter how small it may be, this is never good for a home.

During a home inspection, if any termite damage is found, it will affect the outcome of the home. In most cases, the buyer is told that the seller will fix the problem. Although this may sound good to some buyers that the seller will treat for termites, buyers often wonder.

Of course, it's nice that the seller will pay to have the termite problem treated, which will normally cost around $1,000. Even though the termites will be gone, you have to wonder about the damage to the structure.

In the more severe cases, damage to the structure can cost up to 50 times the cost of the treatment. The last thing you want is to move into a home that you know has been treated for termites.

There could also be latent damage present as well. To determine this, you'll need to have invasive testing performed on the home, which will need to be performed by qualified contractors and specialists. This will help to determine the extent of the damage and the cost of any needed for repairs. This can be very costly, although it's the only way to find and repair any latent damage.

If any type of damage was done to the wooden structure of the home, you may need to get immediate repairs. Some damage may be visible, other types of damage may not be invisible to the naked eye. To find out just how bad the damage is, carpets and rugs will need to be lifted, furniture and appliances moved, walls and ceilings will need to be opened, and even some types of excavation may be needed.

This is the only way to tell the extent of the damages. If you don't inspect every area of the home, you could be moving into a home that has severe structural damage - which can cost you thousands to repair.

If you are renting the home, you'll need to get written documentation from the specialist that details the damage to the home and the cost of repairs.

CHAPTER 5: REASONS TO STAGE YOUR HOME FOR SALE

If you've been thinking of selling your investment house or your home, you should consider taking advantage of home staging.

There are several advantages to home staging, which we will take a look at below.

One of the best things about staged homes is that they typically sell in less time. This is great news for sellers, as these types of homes will sell fast. In most cases, you won't have to worry about your home staying on the market for a long time. Research has shown that staged homes sell nearly 40% faster than other homes on the market.

Staged homes also sell for more money. Homes that are on the market for a long time will normally get lower offers. Buyers will begin to think there is something wrong with the home. Staged homes, on the other hand, don't sit on the market very long. Staged homes draw attention to themselves - resulting in a fast sale.

A staged exterior will also draw viewers. When homebuyers first arrive at a home that is up for sale, they instantly make up their mind whether they should get out and look around. If the yard is staged with flowers and the yard is manicured and properly taken care of, chances are that buyers will want to see more.

If you entice your buyers by showing them how nice the home is outside, they will surely want to know what the home is like on the inside as well.

Once a buyer has stepped inside of the home, they will know within a matter of seconds whether or not he likes the home. You don't want the buyer to feel overwhelmed with clutter or get the wrong impression.

Staging the living rooms and kitchens will also help to sell the home. Buyers love living rooms, which is why you should always make sure that the living room is the centerpiece of your home, and decorate accordingly. Kitchens, on the other hand, is where you should go all out, decorating with fruit and such. You should always make sure that everything is professionally cleaned. Buyers love to see homes that are ready to move-in.

Staged homes will also attract more buyers as well. If a Realtor loves your home, they will want to show it off. Realtor's, will advertise your home more than others, just to get you some attention. This way, you can benefit from a lot of exposure at absolutely no extra cost.

There's no other way to look at it, other than staged homes sell. Staged homes attract more buyers, Realtors, and they give people the feeling of home. When you go out of your way to make the buyer feel that your home is their dream home, they will know it.

Homes that aren't staged may sell, although staged homes sell much faster and for more money. If you've been looking to sell your home, you should look into staging it and get the ball rolling in the right direction. At the bare minimum have your home decluttered and professionally cleaned.

CHAPTER 6: REAL ESTATE INVESTORS OFFER PERKS TO RETAIN TENANTS

What tenant wouldn't love the allure of high-speed Internet and a computer of their own?

This is one of many incentives that investors and property owners are offering to retain or reward long term tenants. Other rewards are just as effective. Property owners feel motivated to offer tenants gift cards after the renewal of a their lease.

Savvy investors realize that an empty house, apartment, mobile home, etc. is money that is being lost each month.

The same savvy investors also realize that by keeping tenants longer will prolong the installation of new carpet, new paint, and other cosmetic repairs that are often required when a dwelling is turned over.

In addition to the costs of these repairs, there is also a time factor, as many of these repairs cannot be completed in a day or two. Bottom line, the time the apartment sits empty, is a lost of income.

If you do have an empty apartment or house there are things you can do to entice renters to sign a lease. One thing that many potential tenants find appealing is offering to allow them to select the color scheme for the walls and flooring.

Most landlord, only permit white walls. Imagine the benefits of not only allowing tenants to select wall colors, but also doing the work for them. This is a great incentive to many renters who love the idea of custom wall paint on the landlord's dime. The ability to have the colors of choice when moving in is a huge bonus.

Another addition that tenants find enticing is having a dishwasher, garbage disposal, built-in microwave, washing machine, or dryer. These luxuries are well worth signing a longer lease and or even paying a little extra for each month. Garages and carports are another great bonus to potential tenants.

There are other enhancements you can make to a property that makes it more appealing to long-term tenants. Some of these would include ceiling fans, a fenced-in yard for children or pets, and free cable television. It is the little touches that often appeal to renters.

By offering your tenants little perks that every other landlord in the area are failing to offer, you will stand out from the rest. You are also creating a 'spoiled' tenant that is content when it's time to renew the lease.

For this reason, he or she is likely to stick around for yet another six months to a year. When the lease expires, a savvy investor can convince the tenant to stay once again.

CHAPTER 7: REAL ESTATE INVESTING FOR THE FIRST TIMER

You have probably read all the information on the market as it relates to real estate investing and you are well aware that many of the world's millionaires made their fortunes in the real estate market.

As a result, I'm sure that you feel ready to throw your hat into the ring and build your real estate portfolio. There is certainly nothing wrong with this as an investment strategy though there are many wrong ways in which an investor can go about the process.

Flipping properties is my field of expertise and a good deal of what will be discussed here in this Chapter. However, some of the information can cross over into rental properties and other types of real estate investments. Even personal property can be a real estate investment. Real estate is one of the few forms of investment in which you can see the changes as they are occurring.

It is truly amazing to watch a property that was once neglected and in a state of disrepair suddenly spark back to life right before your very eyes. There is a lot of work involved in this process.

Keep these things in mind for your first time and you should be well on your way. You should also realize that the first few investments are learning experiences. If you do not achieve the success you were hoping for, you should not give up on the dream all together. Learn from the mistakes you will make along the way as well as the mistakes that others have made. As an investment coach I walk all of my clients through this process start to finish.

Real Estate investing is not an exact science. There is no formula in this business that guarantees success. Even seasoned professionals will find the occasional bump in the road even on a property for which they had high expectations. Unforeseen cost issues happen along the way, such as permit delays and or structural defects. These things are stumbling blocks, but should not be allowed to derail the entire project. When setbacks happen, go back to your original plan, reassess the situation, and create a new plan. The key is, to stick to a plan the entire time and never throw the plan out the window.

Your plan will be your lifeline throughout the project. You need to have a plan and a budget in writing. One great rule of thumb is to set aside double the amount of money you plan for in your budget. This gives you a bit of a safety net for the inevitable things that can go wrong.

You'll encounter issues on almost every flip. Even the seasoned professionals encounter problems.

For your first few investments, it is recommended that you purchase properties that need little more than minor cosmetic repair rather than complete rehabs or renovations. This allows you to get your feet wet without the incredible risk.

These properties represent lower profits but offer lower risk. They also allow you to gain valuable experience and extend capital to invest in other ventures.

Keep your eye on the carrot at the end of the project. Far too many would-be property investors give up just before they reach the point of true; profitability. The goal at end of the project is "Profit."

IN SUMMARY

I leave you with these five Tips!

- Build an investment portfolio that's custom to your tolerance level. Start with a dollar amount you can afford to lose.

- Give a smaller Real Estate firm a shot at your listing. They may be a little more focused on your needs and your listing won't be overlooked.

- Hire a Home Inspector before buying your home. It's the buyer's choice in most states.

- Check with local furniture companies in your area if you consider staging your home. Some will be glad to assist. Consider selling the furniture along with the home!

- Consider using a Fix and Flip Coach like Russ H. Carrington on your first few deals.